The Civil Rights Movement

American history, Volume 8

Michael Johnson

Published by Harmony House Publishing, 2024.

While every precaution has been taken in the preparation of this book, the publisher assumes no responsibility for errors or omissions, or for damages resulting from the use of the information contained herein.

THE CIVIL RIGHTS MOVEMENT

First edition. March 28, 2024.

ISBN: 979-8224314362

Written by Michael Johnson.

Table of Contents

To those who marched, protested, and fought tirelessly for civil rights, this book is dedicated to your courage, resilience, and unwavering commitment to justice. Your sacrifices paved the way for a more equitable society, and your legacy continues to inspire generations. May this book honor your struggles and serve as a reminder of the ongoing fight for equality.

Chapter 1: Prelude to the Movement

The Civil Rights Movement did not emerge in a vacuum but was deeply rooted in the historical context of racial oppression and resistance that spanned centuries. This chapter explores the complex historical landscape leading up to the Civil Rights Movement, examining pivotal events, legislation, and key figures that laid the groundwork for the eventual struggle for equality.

Reconstruction and Its Aftermath

Following the end of the Civil War in 1865, the United States entered a period known as Reconstruction. This era marked a significant attempt to rebuild the nation and address the issues of slavery and racial inequality. The Reconstruction Amendments, including the 13th, 14th, and 15th Amendments to the Constitution, were ratified during this time, abolishing slavery, granting citizenship and equal protection under the law to all citizens, and prohibiting the denial of voting rights based on race.

However, Reconstruction was short-lived, and the promises of equality and justice for African Americans were soon undermined by the rise of Jim Crow laws and the resurgence of white supremacy. Southern states enacted a series of discriminatory laws and practices aimed at segregating and disenfranchising African Americans, effectively institutionalizing racial segregation and inequality.

Jim Crow Laws and Racial Segregation

Jim Crow laws, named after a minstrel character that mocked African Americans, enforced racial segregation in public facilities, transportation, schools, and other aspects of daily life. These laws perpetuated racial discrimination and created a system of separate and unequal treatment for African Americans, denying them basic rights and opportunities afforded to white citizens.

Under Jim Crow, African Americans faced systemic oppression and violence, including lynching, economic exploitation, and limited access to education and employment opportunities. The pervasive nature of racial segregation and discrimination entrenched the idea of white supremacy and reinforced the social hierarchy based on race.

Plessy v. Ferguson and the "Separate but Equal" Doctrine

In 1896, the Supreme Court issued its landmark decision in Plessy v. Ferguson, which upheld the constitutionality of racial segregation under the doctrine of "separate but equal." The case originated from Homer Plessy, an African American man who challenged Louisiana's Separate Car Act, which required segregated railway cars.

The Court's ruling sanctioned segregation and provided legal justification for discriminatory practices, further entrenching racial inequality in American society. Despite the inherent injustice of segregation, the "separate but equal" doctrine remained the law of the land for decades, legitimizing the segregationist policies and practices that would later be challenged by the Civil Rights Movement.

The Birth of Civil Rights Organizations

Amidst the oppressive climate of Jim Crow and segregation, African Americans began organizing and mobilizing for civil rights and equality. One of the earliest organizations to advocate for racial justice was the National Association for the Advancement of Colored People (NAACP), founded in 1909 by a multiracial group of activists, including W.E.B. Du Bois, Ida B. Wells, and Mary White Ovington.

The NAACP sought to combat racial discrimination through legal means, using litigation and advocacy to challenge segregation and secure civil rights protections for African Americans. Over the years, the NAACP played a pivotal role in landmark Supreme Court cases and legislative battles, laying the groundwork for the eventual dismantling of segregation and the advancement of civil rights.

Key Figures and Events

Several key figures emerged during this prelude to the Civil Rights Movement, whose actions and contributions paved the way for future activism and resistance:

- **Booker T. Washington**: A prominent African American educator and leader, Washington advocated for vocational training and economic self-sufficiency for African Americans. His philosophy of gradualism and accommodation contrasted with the more radical approaches of other civil rights leaders but nonetheless influenced the trajectory of African American activism.

- **W.E.B. Du Bois**: A leading intellectual and civil rights activist, Du Bois was a co-founder of the NAACP and editor of its influential publication, The Crisis. Du Bois championed the rights of African Americans and called for immediate social and political equality, challenging Booker T. Washington's accommodationist approach.

- **Ida B. Wells**: A journalist, educator, and civil rights activist, Wells was a fierce advocate against lynching and racial violence. Her investigative reporting exposed the brutality of lynching and galvanized public outrage, making her a pioneering figure in the fight for racial justice.

- **Marcus Garvey**: A Jamaican-born activist and leader of the Pan-African movement, Garvey founded the Universal Negro Improvement Association (UNIA) and advocated for black nationalism and self-determination. Garvey's message of black pride and empowerment resonated with millions of African Americans and laid the groundwork for later movements such as Black Power.

- **The Atlanta Compromise**: In 1895, Booker T. Washington delivered his famous Atlanta Compromise speech, in which he called for African Americans to temporarily accept segregation and disenfranchisement while focusing on economic advancement and education. The speech sparked debate within the African American community about the most effective strategies for achieving equality.

These key figures and events, along with countless others, set the stage for the Civil Rights Movement, planting the seeds of resistance and laying the groundwork for the monumental struggles that would follow. Despite the formidable obstacles of segregation and discrimination, African Americans continued to resist and organize, laying the foundation for a movement that would ultimately transform the nation.

Chapter 2: Brown v. Board of Education and the Legal Battle for Equality

The landmark Supreme Court case Brown v. Board of Education stands as one of the most significant legal victories in the history of the Civil Rights Movement. This chapter delves into the intricacies of the case, the legal strategies employed by Thurgood Marshall and the NAACP Legal Defense Fund, and the far-reaching impact of the Brown decision on subsequent civil rights activism.

Background of Segregation in Education

Segregation in public education was deeply entrenched in the United States long before the Brown case. Following the end of Reconstruction, Southern states implemented laws and policies that enforced racial segregation in schools, denying African American children access to the same educational opportunities as their white counterparts. These "separate but equal" facilities were anything but equal, perpetuating racial inequality and limiting the prospects of African American students.

The legal doctrine established in Plessy v. Ferguson (1896), which upheld the constitutionality of racial segregation under the guise of "separate but equal," provided the legal foundation for discriminatory practices in education and other areas of public life. As a result, African American children attended underfunded, overcrowded schools with inferior resources and facilities, perpetuating the cycle of poverty and inequality.

The Origins of Brown v. Board of Education

The case of Brown v. Board of Education originated from a series of lawsuits challenging school segregation in several states, including Kansas, South Carolina, Virginia, Delaware, and the District of Columbia. Oliver Brown, a welder and assistant pastor in Topeka, Kansas, became the namesake plaintiff in the Kansas case after his daughter, Linda Brown, was denied admission to the nearby white elementary school due to her race.

Thurgood Marshall, then the chief counsel for the NAACP Legal Defense Fund (LDF), spearheaded the legal strategy to challenge segregation in education. Marshall and his team strategically selected cases from different regions of the country to demonstrate the widespread nature of segregation and its inherent injustice.

Legal Strategies and Arguments

Thurgood Marshall and the LDF employed a multifaceted legal strategy to challenge segregation in education, drawing on both constitutional principles and social science evidence to make their case. Central to their argument was the assertion that segregation in public schools violated the Equal Protection Clause of the 14th Amendment, which guarantees equal treatment under the law.

Marshall and his team presented evidence to the Supreme Court demonstrating the psychological harm inflicted on African American children by segregation, citing research that showed the detrimental effects of racial segregation on self-esteem and academic achievement. They argued that segregation perpetuated feelings of inferiority among African American students and contributed to the perpetuation of racial stereotypes and prejudices.

In addition to constitutional arguments, Marshall also emphasized the importance of the Court's moral authority in shaping the nation's understanding of justice and equality. He urged the justices to consider the broader implications of their decision and to recognize the fundamental humanity and dignity of all individuals, regardless of race.

The Brown Decision and Its Impact

On May 17, 1954, the Supreme Court handed down its unanimous decision in Brown v. Board of Education, declaring that segregation in public schools was unconstitutional and overturning the precedent established in Plessy v. Ferguson. Chief Justice Earl Warren delivered the Court's opinion, stating that "separate educational facilities are inherently unequal" and that segregation had a detrimental effect on the education and personal development of African American children.

The Brown decision marked a watershed moment in the struggle for civil rights, striking a blow to the legal foundation of segregation and providing a powerful impetus for subsequent activism and legal challenges. The ruling galvanized civil rights activists and provided a legal precedent for challenging segregation in other areas of public life, including transportation, housing, and employment.

Implementation and Resistance

Despite the Supreme Court's ruling in Brown, the process of desegregating public schools proved to be a long and contentious battle. Many Southern states resisted the Court's decision, implementing various tactics to delay or circumvent desegregation, including "massive resistance" laws, school closings, and white flight to private academies.

Thurgood Marshall and the NAACP Legal Defense Fund continued to litigate cases to enforce the Brown decision and dismantle segregation in schools. The LDF's efforts were met with fierce opposition from segregationist politicians and white supremacist groups, but they persevered, securing additional victories in the courts and gradually breaking down the barriers of segregation.

Legacy of Brown v. Board of Education

The legacy of Brown v. Board of Education extends far beyond its immediate impact on school segregation. The case paved the way for subsequent civil rights legislation, including the Civil Rights Act of 1964 and the Voting Rights Act of 1965, which sought to dismantle other forms of racial discrimination and ensure equal rights for all Americans.

Brown also inspired a new generation of activists and leaders who would carry forward the struggle for civil rights and social justice. The decision challenged the nation to confront the legacy of racial segregation and inequality and to strive toward a more inclusive and equitable society.

In conclusion, Brown v. Board of Education represented a pivotal moment in the history of the Civil Rights Movement, signaling the beginning of the end of legal segregation and providing a powerful example of the potential of law and litigation to effect social change. Thurgood Marshall and the NAACP Legal

Defense Fund's legal strategies and arguments laid the groundwork for future victories in the fight for equality, inspiring generations of activists to continue the struggle for justice and fairness.

Chapter 3: Montgomery Bus Boycott and the Rise of Martin Luther King Jr.

The Montgomery Bus Boycott, ignited by Rosa Parks' courageous act of defiance, marked a pivotal moment in the Civil Rights Movement and propelled Martin Luther King Jr. into the national spotlight. This chapter provides a detailed account of the boycott, explores King's emergence as a central figure in the movement, and analyzes the strategies employed during the boycott's duration, which galvanized nationwide support for desegregation.

Rosa Parks and the Catalyst for Change

On December 1, 1955, Rosa Parks, a 42-year-old African American seamstress and activist, boarded a city bus in Montgomery, Alabama, after a long day at work. As the bus filled with passengers, Parks took a seat in the designated "colored" section near the middle. When the bus driver demanded that Parks give up her seat to a white passenger, she refused, sparking her arrest and igniting a wave of protest and resistance.

Parks' arrest was not an isolated incident but rather the culmination of years of systemic racism and segregation on Montgomery's buses. African American passengers were required to sit in the back of the bus and give up their seats to white passengers if the white section became full, reinforcing the dehumanizing segregation policies of the Jim Crow era.

The Birth of the Montgomery Improvement Association

Following Rosa Parks' arrest, African American leaders in Montgomery, including E.D. Nixon and Jo Ann Robinson, sprang into action to organize a boycott of the city's buses. On December 5, 1955, they formed the Montgomery Improvement Association (MIA), with Martin Luther King Jr., a young pastor at Dexter Avenue Baptist Church, elected as its president. The MIA's primary objective was to challenge segregation on Montgomery's buses and demand equal treatment for African American passengers.

Martin Luther King Jr.'s involvement in the boycott would thrust him into a leadership role and provide a platform for his message of nonviolent resistance and social justice. At just 26 years old, King emerged as a charismatic and eloquent spokesperson for the Civil Rights Movement, rallying the African American community and inspiring them to continue the struggle for equality.

Strategies of Nonviolent Resistance

The Montgomery Bus Boycott was characterized by its commitment to nonviolent resistance, inspired by the teachings of Mahatma Gandhi and Christian principles of love and forgiveness. The MIA and its supporters organized a coordinated campaign of economic protest, urging African Americans to boycott the city's buses until segregation was abolished.

To sustain the boycott, alternative transportation networks were established, including carpools, walking groups, and even a fleet of private cars operated by volunteers. The African American community demonstrated remarkable solidarity and resilience, enduring long walks to work, harassment, and threats of violence in pursuit of justice.

Legal Challenges and Court Battles

As the boycott persisted, the Montgomery city government and bus company attempted to quash the protest through legal means, obtaining injunctions against the boycott and arresting leaders of the movement. However, Martin Luther King Jr. and the MIA remained undeterred, continuing to advocate for their cause through peaceful means and legal channels.

The legal battle culminated in the landmark Supreme Court case Browder v. Gayle, which ultimately declared Montgomery's segregated bus system unconstitutional. On November 13, 1956, the Supreme Court affirmed the lower court's ruling, ordering Montgomery to desegregate its buses and marking a significant victory for the Civil Rights Movement.

Nationwide Impact and Legacy

The Montgomery Bus Boycott captured the attention of the nation and inspired similar acts of resistance and protest against segregation in other cities and states. The success of the boycott demonstrated the power of nonviolent protest and grassroots organizing to effect social change, inspiring future generations of activists and leaders.

Moreover, the boycott elevated Martin Luther King Jr. to national prominence and solidified his position as a leading voice in the struggle for civil rights. King's eloquence, moral clarity, and commitment to nonviolence resonated with people across the country, earning him widespread admiration and support.

The Montgomery Bus Boycott's legacy extends far beyond its immediate impact on desegregation. It served as a catalyst for the broader Civil Rights Movement, energizing activists and galvanizing public opinion against segregation and racial injustice. The boycott's success demonstrated the power of collective action and inspired future generations to continue the fight for equality and justice for all.

Chapter 4: Student Activism: Sit-Ins, Freedom Rides, and the Youth Movement

The Civil Rights Movement of the 1950s and 1960s was greatly energized and propelled forward by the involvement of young people, particularly college students, who played a pivotal role in challenging segregation and advocating for civil rights. This chapter explores the significant contributions of student activists through sit-ins, Freedom Rides, and the formation of organizations like the Student Nonviolent Coordinating Committee (SNCC). It examines the challenges faced by these young activists and their enduring impact on the movement for racial equality.

The Rise of Student Activism

In the early 1960s, a new wave of activism emerged within the Civil Rights Movement, driven largely by the energy and idealism of college students. Frustrated by the slow pace of change and inspired by the successes of the Montgomery Bus Boycott and other grassroots campaigns, students across the South began to organize and mobilize for civil rights.

Many of these students were inspired by the teachings of nonviolent resistance espoused by leaders like Martin Luther King Jr. and the principles of direct action championed by organizations like the Southern Christian Leadership Conference (SCLC) and the Fellowship of Reconciliation (FOR). They saw themselves as heirs to the legacy of earlier civil rights struggles and were determined to continue the fight for justice and equality.

Sit-Ins: Challenging Segregation at Lunch Counters

One of the most iconic forms of student activism during this period was the sit-in, a nonviolent protest tactic aimed at challenging segregation in public accommodations. The sit-ins began on February 1, 1960, when four African American college students from North Carolina Agricultural and Technical State University—Ezell Blair Jr., David Richmond, Franklin McCain, and Joseph

McNeil—sat down at a whites-only lunch counter at a Woolworth's store in Greensboro, North Carolina.

Despite being refused service, the students remained seated at the lunch counter, peacefully occupying the space and refusing to leave until closing time. Their act of defiance sparked a wave of sit-ins across the South, as students in cities like Nashville, Atlanta, and Birmingham followed their example and staged similar protests at segregated lunch counters.

The sit-ins were met with hostility and violence from segregationists, who physically assaulted the protesters and arrested them for trespassing and disorderly conduct. However, the students remained steadfast in their commitment to nonviolence, drawing widespread attention to the injustice of segregation and inspiring others to join the struggle.

Formation of the Student Nonviolent Coordinating Committee (SNCC)

Out of the sit-in movement emerged the Student Nonviolent Coordinating Committee (SNCC), a grassroots organization comprised primarily of young activists committed to nonviolent direct action and community organizing. Formed in April 1960 at a conference organized by Ella Baker, a veteran civil rights organizer, SNCC sought to mobilize and empower African American communities to challenge segregation and discrimination.

SNCC played a central role in coordinating sit-ins, Freedom Rides, voter registration drives, and other acts of civil disobedience throughout the South. The organization adopted a decentralized structure, emphasizing the importance of local leadership and grassroots organizing, and worked closely with other civil rights groups to advance the cause of racial equality.

Freedom Rides: Testing Segregation on Interstate Transportation

Building on the success of the sit-in movement, student activists launched the Freedom Rides in 1961, a series of integrated bus journeys aimed at challenging segregation on interstate transportation. Organized by the Congress of Racial Equality (CORE) and supported by SNCC and other civil rights organizations, the Freedom Rides sought to test the enforcement of recent Supreme Court rulings prohibiting segregation in interstate travel.

The Freedom Riders, both black and white, faced violent resistance from segregationists as they traveled through the South, encountering mob attacks, arrests, and imprisonment. Despite the dangers, the Riders remained committed to their mission, drawing international attention to the brutality of segregation and putting pressure on the federal government to enforce desegregation laws.

Key Student Leaders and Their Contributions

Several key student leaders emerged during this period, whose courage and leadership were instrumental in advancing the goals of the Civil Rights Movement:

- **John Lewis**: A young activist from Troy, Alabama, John Lewis became a prominent leader within SNCC and played a key role in organizing the Freedom Rides. Lewis would later become a congressman and a leading figure in the ongoing struggle for civil rights and social justice.

- **Diane Nash**: A student at Fisk University in Nashville, Tennessee, Diane Nash played a central role in organizing sit-ins and coordinating the Freedom Rides. Her fearless leadership and commitment to nonviolence were instrumental in shaping the tactics and strategies of the movement.

- **Bob Moses**: As a field secretary for SNCC, Bob Moses played a crucial role in organizing voter registration drives and grassroots organizing efforts in Mississippi. His work laid the foundation for the Mississippi Freedom Summer of 1964, a massive voter registration campaign aimed at empowering African American voters in the Deep South.

Challenges and Contributions of Young Activists

Despite their idealism and determination, young activists faced numerous challenges and obstacles in their efforts to challenge segregation and discrimination. They were met with violence and intimidation from segregationist forces, as well as resistance from within their own communities and institutions.

Moreover, many young activists struggled with the demands of activism, balancing their commitments to the movement with their academic responsibilities and personal lives. They faced the risk of arrest, expulsion from school, and violence from vigilante groups, yet they remained resolute in their commitment to justice and equality.

Despite these challenges, young activists made significant contributions to the Civil Rights Movement, bringing energy, creativity, and a sense of urgency to the struggle. Their willingness to put their bodies on the line and their dedication to nonviolent resistance inspired countless others to join the movement and helped to catalyze social change.

Legacy of Student Activism

The legacy of student activism during the Civil Rights Movement is profound and enduring, shaping not only the course of the struggle for racial equality but also the broader landscape of social justice and activism in America. The sit-ins, Freedom Rides, and grassroots organizing efforts led by young activists laid the groundwork for future movements for civil rights, women's rights, LGBTQ+ rights, and environmental justice.

Moreover, the leadership and courage demonstrated by young activists like John Lewis, Diane Nash, and Bob Moses continue to inspire new generations of activists and organizers to stand up for justice and equality. Their contributions serve as a reminder of the power of young people to effect change and to challenge injustice wherever it exists.

Chapter 5: Birmingham Campaign and the Power of Nonviolent Resistance

The Birmingham Campaign of 1963 stands as a watershed moment in the Civil Rights Movement, showcasing the power of nonviolent protest tactics in confronting segregation and systemic racism. This chapter provides a detailed analysis of the Birmingham Campaign, including the strategies employed, the confrontations with segregationist authorities, and the pivotal role of the media in exposing violence against demonstrators. Furthermore, it explores the campaign's impact on national consciousness and its role in catalyzing the passage of civil rights legislation.

Setting the Stage: Birmingham, Alabama

Birmingham, Alabama, was known as "Bombingham" due to its reputation for racial violence and segregationist policies. The city's strict segregation laws and entrenched racism made it a focal point for civil rights activism, drawing the attention of national civil rights leaders and organizations.

Led by the Reverend Fred Shuttlesworth, the Alabama Christian Movement for Human Rights (ACMHR) had been organizing protests and demonstrations against segregation in Birmingham for years, but progress was slow, and efforts were met with violent resistance from local authorities and white supremacists.

The Leadership of Martin Luther King Jr.

In early 1963, Martin Luther King Jr. and the Southern Christian Leadership Conference (SCLC) joined forces with local activists to launch a coordinated campaign of nonviolent direct action in Birmingham. King recognized Birmingham's significance as a battleground for civil rights and saw an opportunity to bring national attention to the struggle for racial equality.

King's leadership was instrumental in shaping the strategy and tactics of the Birmingham Campaign. Drawing on the principles of nonviolent resistance and civil disobedience, King and his fellow organizers sought to challenge segregation and discrimination through peaceful protest and moral persuasion.

Nonviolent Protest Tactics

Central to the Birmingham Campaign was the use of nonviolent protest tactics, including sit-ins, marches, and boycotts, aimed at disrupting business as usual and highlighting the injustice of segregation. Demonstrators were trained in the principles of nonviolence and were instructed to remain calm and disciplined in the face of provocation and violence.

One of the most iconic moments of the campaign was the Children's Crusade, in which hundreds of young people, some as young as six years old, participated in marches and demonstrations against segregation. The images of children being arrested and attacked by police shocked the nation and drew widespread condemnation of Birmingham's segregationist policies.

Confrontations with Segregationist Authorities

The Birmingham Campaign was met with fierce opposition from segregationist authorities, who sought to maintain the status quo through violence and intimidation. Birmingham Police Commissioner Eugene "Bull" Connor ordered the use of high-pressure fire hoses and police dogs against peaceful demonstrators, resulting in scenes of brutality and chaos that were captured by the media and broadcast around the world.

The violence perpetrated by law enforcement against unarmed protesters sparked outrage and condemnation from civil rights leaders, religious leaders, and public figures across the country. The images of African American men, women, and children being attacked by police resonated with people of conscience and galvanized support for the civil rights movement.

Role of the Media

The Birmingham Campaign was a turning point in the relationship between the civil rights movement and the media. Journalists and photographers from national and international news outlets descended on Birmingham to cover the protests and document the violence against demonstrators.

The images and footage captured by the media, including the iconic photographs of police dogs attacking peaceful protesters, brought the reality of segregation and racial violence into living rooms across America. The coverage of the Birmingham Campaign played a crucial role in shaping public opinion and mobilizing support for civil rights legislation.

Impact on National Consciousness and Legislation

The Birmingham Campaign had a profound impact on national consciousness and public opinion, sparking a moral awakening and mobilizing support for civil rights legislation. The images of violence and injustice in Birmingham helped to galvanize public outrage and pressure President John F. Kennedy and Congress to take action.

In June 1963, President Kennedy delivered a nationally televised address in which he called for the passage of comprehensive civil rights legislation, citing the moral imperative of ending segregation and racial discrimination. Later that year, Congress passed the Civil Rights Act of 1964, which outlawed segregation in public accommodations and employment discrimination based on race, color, religion, sex, or national origin.

Legacy of the Birmingham Campaign

The Birmingham Campaign left an indelible mark on the Civil Rights Movement and the struggle for racial equality in America. It demonstrated the power of nonviolent resistance in confronting injustice and inspired future generations of activists and organizers to continue the fight for civil rights and social justice.

Moreover, the Birmingham Campaign helped to dismantle the myth of racial superiority and exposed the brutality of segregation and systemic racism. It challenged Americans to confront the reality of racial injustice and to work towards creating a more just and equitable society for all.

In conclusion, the Birmingham Campaign stands as a testament to the courage and resilience of those who fought for freedom and equality in the face of violence and oppression. It serves as a reminder of the transformative power of nonviolent resistance and the enduring legacy of the Civil Rights Movement in the ongoing struggle for justice and equality.

Chapter 6: March on Washington and the Dream of Equality

The March on Washington for Jobs and Freedom, held on August 28, 1963, stands as one of the most iconic moments in American history and a defining moment in the Civil Rights Movement. This chapter provides a detailed overview of the historic march, examines Martin Luther King Jr.'s iconic "I Have a Dream" speech and its resonance within the movement, and analyzes the influence of the march on public opinion and legislative action, including the passage of the Civil Rights Act of 1964.

The Context of the March

In the early 1960s, the Civil Rights Movement was at a critical juncture, with ongoing struggles for desegregation, voting rights, and economic justice. Despite significant victories such as the desegregation of interstate transportation and the passage of the Civil Rights Act of 1964, deep-seated racial inequality persisted, particularly in the South.

Against this backdrop, civil rights leaders and organizations began planning a massive demonstration in Washington, D.C., to demand jobs, freedom, and an end to racial discrimination. The March on Washington for Jobs and Freedom was envisioned as a peaceful, multiracial gathering to mobilize public support and pressure the federal government to enact meaningful civil rights legislation.

Organizing the March

The planning and coordination of the March on Washington involved a diverse coalition of civil rights organizations, labor unions, religious groups, and grassroots activists. A. Philip Randolph, the veteran labor leader and civil rights activist, played a central role in organizing the march and served as its chief organizer.

Under Randolph's leadership, the march's organizers sought to ensure that it was inclusive and representative of the broader civil rights movement, with participation from diverse communities and regions across the country. They also worked to secure the support of political leaders, including President John F. Kennedy, who initially expressed reservations about the march but eventually endorsed it.

The "Big Six" and the Goals of the March

The planning and coordination of the March on Washington were overseen by a group of civil rights leaders known as the "Big Six." This coalition included leaders such as Martin Luther King Jr., John Lewis, A. Philip Randolph, Whitney Young, Roy Wilkins, and James Farmer, who represented a cross-section of the civil rights movement.

The goals of the march were outlined in a list of demands known as the "March on Washington for Jobs and Freedom" platform. These demands included comprehensive civil rights legislation, desegregation of public schools, an end to racial discrimination in employment, and the enactment of a federal jobs program to address economic inequality.

The "I Have a Dream" Speech

The highlight of the March on Washington was Martin Luther King Jr.'s iconic "I Have a Dream" speech, delivered from the steps of the Lincoln Memorial to a crowd of more than 250,000 demonstrators. King's speech articulated the hopes and aspirations of millions of Americans for racial equality and justice and became one of the defining moments of the Civil Rights Movement.

In his speech, King called for an end to racial segregation and discrimination, invoking the principles of freedom, justice, and equality enshrined in the Declaration of Independence and the Constitution. He spoke of his dream of a future where people would be judged not by the color of their skin but by the content of their character, inspiring generations of Americans to continue the fight for civil rights and social justice.

Resonance and Impact of the Speech

King's "I Have a Dream" speech resonated deeply with the American public and had a profound impact on the civil rights movement and the broader struggle for racial equality. The imagery and rhetoric of the speech captured the imagination of millions of Americans, transcending racial and ideological divides and inspiring renewed commitment to the cause of civil rights.

The speech also had a significant influence on public opinion and political action, helping to mobilize support for civil rights legislation and galvanize public pressure on the federal government to address racial injustice. President Kennedy, who had initially been cautious about supporting the march, was moved by King's speech and later cited it as a factor in his decision to propose comprehensive civil rights legislation.

Legacy of the March

The March on Washington for Jobs and Freedom left a lasting legacy that continues to resonate to this day. It demonstrated the power of nonviolent protest and mass mobilization to effect social change and highlighted the importance of coalition-building and grassroots organizing in the struggle for civil rights.

Moreover, the march helped to elevate the issue of civil rights to the top of the national agenda and paved the way for the passage of the Civil Rights Act of 1964, which outlawed racial segregation and discrimination in public accommodations, employment, and voting. The march also inspired future generations of activists and organizers to continue the fight for justice and equality.

In conclusion, the March on Washington for Jobs and Freedom was a pivotal moment in the Civil Rights Movement and a testament to the courage, determination, and vision of those who participated in it. It served as a beacon of hope and inspiration for millions of Americans and helped to advance the cause of racial equality and justice in America.

Chapter 7: Voting Rights Struggle: Selma to Montgomery March

The struggle for voting rights was a central focus of the Civil Rights Movement, particularly in the South, where African Americans faced systemic barriers to political participation and representation. This chapter provides a detailed examination of the voting rights challenges faced by African Americans, a thorough account of the Selma to Montgomery March led by John Lewis and other civil rights leaders, and an analysis of the significance of the Voting Rights Act of 1965 in ensuring African American enfranchisement.

The Context of Voting Rights Challenges

In the years following Reconstruction, African Americans in the South were systematically disenfranchised through a combination of discriminatory laws and practices, including poll taxes, literacy tests, and intimidation tactics. These barriers to voting were designed to maintain white supremacy and political control over African American communities, effectively denying them their constitutional right to participate in the democratic process.

Despite the passage of the 15th Amendment in 1870, which prohibited the denial of voting rights based on race, African Americans in the South continued to face discrimination and violence when attempting to exercise their right to vote. The efforts of civil rights activists to challenge these barriers and secure voting rights for African Americans became a central focus of the Civil Rights Movement in the 1950s and 1960s.

The Selma to Montgomery March

One of the most iconic events in the struggle for voting rights was the Selma to Montgomery March, a series of marches organized by civil rights leaders in Alabama in 1965. The marches were prompted by the ongoing disenfranchisement of African American voters in Selma and other parts of the state, despite the passage of federal legislation aimed at protecting voting rights.

Led by John Lewis, Hosea Williams, and other leaders of the Southern Christian Leadership Conference (SCLC) and the Student Nonviolent Coordinating Committee (SNCC), the marches sought to draw attention to the injustices faced by African American voters and to pressure state and federal authorities to take action.

Bloody Sunday and the Turn of Events

The first attempt to march from Selma to Montgomery, on March 7, 1965, was met with brutal violence by state and local law enforcement officers. As the marchers attempted to cross the Edmund Pettus Bridge, they were confronted by Alabama state troopers and local police who unleashed tear gas and brutally beat the peaceful demonstrators.

The violence of "Bloody Sunday," as it came to be known, shocked the nation and galvanized support for the voting rights movement. Images of the marchers being attacked by police were broadcast on television screens across the country, prompting outrage and condemnation from civil rights leaders, elected officials, and ordinary citizens.

Continued Resistance and Marches

Despite the violence of Bloody Sunday, the marchers remained undeterred in their commitment to secure voting rights for African Americans. Under the leadership of Dr. Martin Luther King Jr. and other civil rights leaders, a second march was organized, this time with federal court protection and a larger contingent of marchers.

On March 9, 1965, the marchers set out once again from Selma, this time led by Dr. King and accompanied by thousands of supporters from across the country. The marchers walked in solidarity, singing freedom songs and carrying banners calling for voting rights and racial justice.

The Triumph of the March

After a series of tense negotiations with state and federal authorities, the marchers finally reached their destination in Montgomery on March 25, 1965, marking a triumphant conclusion to their journey. The Selma to Montgomery March had succeeded in drawing national attention to the issue of voting rights and mobilizing public support for legislative action.

The passage of the Voting Rights Act of 1965, signed into law by President Lyndon B. Johnson on August 6, 1965, was a direct result of the Selma to Montgomery March and the broader voting rights movement. The act prohibited racial discrimination in voting, including literacy tests and other voter suppression tactics, and authorized federal oversight of election practices in states with a history of voter discrimination.

Legacy of the Selma to Montgomery March

The Selma to Montgomery March stands as a defining moment in the struggle for voting rights and a testament to the courage and resilience of those who participated in it. The marchers' willingness to risk their lives and endure violence and intimidation in the pursuit of justice helped to secure voting rights for millions of African Americans and paved the way for greater political participation and representation.

Moreover, the Selma to Montgomery March inspired future generations of activists and organizers to continue the fight for civil rights and social justice. The legacy of the march lives on in the ongoing struggle to protect and expand voting rights for all Americans and to ensure that every citizen has an equal voice in the democratic process.

Chapter 8: Northern Front: Urban Riots and the Fight for Fair Housing

While much attention in the Civil Rights Movement has focused on the struggle for racial equality in the South, significant challenges also existed in Northern cities. This chapter delves into the civil rights struggles in Northern cities, particularly focusing on issues of housing discrimination and police brutality. It examines urban riots as expressions of frustration and demands for equality, and analyzes legislative responses to urban unrest and efforts to address systemic racism in the North.

Context of Civil Rights Struggles in Northern Cities

In the post-World War II era, millions of African Americans migrated from the rural South to Northern cities in search of economic opportunities and escape from Jim Crow segregation. However, they encountered a different form of discrimination and segregation in the North, including housing discrimination, job discrimination, and unequal access to education and public services.

Housing discrimination was particularly pervasive, as African Americans faced restrictive covenants, redlining, and outright exclusion from white neighborhoods. These discriminatory practices limited African Americans' housing options, perpetuated residential segregation, and contributed to entrenched poverty and inequality in Northern cities.

Police Brutality and Civil Rights Activism

In addition to housing discrimination, African Americans in Northern cities also faced police brutality and harassment. Police departments were often complicit in enforcing segregation and maintaining white supremacy, targeting African American communities with excessive force and discriminatory policing practices.

Civil rights activists in the North, inspired by the tactics of their Southern counterparts, organized protests and demonstrations to challenge police brutality and demand accountability from law enforcement agencies.

Organizations like the Congress of Racial Equality (CORE), the NAACP, and local grassroots groups played a central role in mobilizing communities and advocating for police reform.

Urban Riots: Expressions of Frustration

The frustrations and grievances of African Americans in Northern cities boiled over in a series of urban riots that erupted in the 1960s. Sparked by incidents of police brutality, racial discrimination, and economic inequality, these riots were expressions of pent-up anger and demands for justice and equality.

One of the most infamous riots occurred in the Watts neighborhood of Los Angeles in 1965, following an altercation between police officers and residents. The riot lasted six days and resulted in 34 deaths, over 1,000 injuries, and millions of dollars in property damage. Similar riots occurred in cities across the country, including Detroit, Newark, and Chicago, highlighting the deep-seated social and economic disparities facing African American communities.

Legislative Responses and Efforts to Address Systemic Racism

The urban riots of the 1960s prompted a national reckoning with issues of racial injustice and inequality in America. In response to mounting pressure from civil rights activists and public outcry over the riots, federal and local governments began to take action to address systemic racism and inequality in Northern cities.

One significant legislative response was the passage of the Fair Housing Act of 1968, which prohibited discrimination in housing based on race, color, religion, sex, or national origin. The act aimed to dismantle segregation and promote fair housing opportunities for all Americans, regardless of race or ethnicity.

Challenges and Ongoing Struggles

Despite legislative victories and efforts to address systemic racism, challenges persist in Northern cities, as racial inequality and segregation continue to shape urban landscapes. African American communities still face disparities in access to housing, education, healthcare, and economic opportunity, perpetuating cycles of poverty and marginalization.

Moreover, issues of police brutality and racial profiling remain prevalent, as evidenced by high-profile cases of police violence against African Americans in cities like New York, Chicago, and Baltimore. Civil rights activists continue to push for police reform and accountability, advocating for measures to address racial bias and improve community-police relations.

Conclusion: Continuing the Fight for Equality

The struggle for racial equality in Northern cities is an ongoing battle that requires sustained effort and commitment from policymakers, community leaders, and ordinary citizens. Addressing systemic racism and dismantling barriers to opportunity and justice requires comprehensive solutions that address the root causes of inequality and discrimination.

By confronting housing discrimination, police brutality, and economic inequality head-on, we can move closer to realizing the promise of equality and justice for all Americans. The legacy of the Civil Rights Movement serves as a guiding light in this ongoing struggle, inspiring us to continue the fight for a more equitable and inclusive society.

Chapter 9: Black Power and the Evolution of the Movement

The Black Power movement emerged in the late 1960s as a powerful and influential force within the broader Civil Rights Movement. Fueled by a deep sense of frustration with the slow pace of progress and ongoing racial injustice, the Black Power movement emphasized racial pride, self-determination, and community empowerment. This chapter provides an in-depth exploration of the Black Power movement, including its origins, key figures such as Stokely Carmichael and the Black Panther Party, and its impact on the trajectory of the Civil Rights Movement.

Origins of the Black Power Movement

The roots of the Black Power movement can be traced back to the frustrations and disillusionment experienced by African Americans in the aftermath of the Civil Rights Movement. Despite significant legislative victories and advances in civil rights, systemic racism and inequality persisted, particularly in Northern cities where African Americans faced discrimination in housing, employment, and education.

The term "Black Power" was popularized by civil rights leader Stokely Carmichael, who first used it during a rally in Greenwood, Mississippi, in June 1966. Carmichael called for African Americans to assert their political and economic power and to embrace their cultural heritage and identity in the face of white supremacy and oppression.

Principles of Black Power

At its core, the Black Power movement emphasized self-determination, self-defense, and solidarity among African Americans. It rejected the integrationist approach of the Civil Rights Movement in favor of a more radical and assertive stance that called for black autonomy and control over their own communities.

Central to the ideology of Black Power was the concept of "Black is Beautiful," which sought to celebrate and affirm African American culture, heritage, and identity. Black Power activists advocated for pride in one's racial identity and sought to challenge white supremacist notions of beauty and worthiness.

Key Figures of the Black Power Movement

Several key figures emerged as leaders of the Black Power movement, each contributing to its development and shaping its trajectory:

- **Stokely Carmichael**: As chairman of the Student Nonviolent Coordinating Committee (SNCC), Stokely Carmichael played a central role in popularizing the concept of Black Power. His fiery speeches and uncompromising stance against racism made him a prominent figure in the movement.

- **Malcolm X**: Although not a formal leader of the Black Power movement, Malcolm X's advocacy for black self-defense and his critique of white supremacy influenced the ideology and tactics of Black Power activists. His emphasis on black pride and self-reliance resonated with many African Americans seeking liberation from oppression.

- **The Black Panther Party**: Founded in Oakland, California, in 1966 by Huey P. Newton and Bobby Seale, the Black Panther Party was one of the most visible and influential organizations of the Black Power movement. The Panthers advocated for armed self-defense, community empowerment, and revolutionary change, and provided social services such as free breakfast programs and health clinics in African American communities.

Impact on the Civil Rights Movement

The emergence of the Black Power movement had a profound impact on the trajectory of the Civil Rights Movement, reshaping its goals, tactics, and strategies. While the Civil Rights Movement focused primarily on legal and political reforms aimed at ending segregation and securing equal rights under the law, the Black Power movement sought to address the deeper roots of racism and inequality in American society.

Black Power activists challenged the moderate leadership of the Civil Rights Movement, arguing that integration and nonviolence were insufficient to address the structural and systemic racism that pervaded American society. Instead, they called for a more radical and militant approach that prioritized black liberation and self-determination.

Challenges and Controversies

The Black Power movement faced criticism and opposition from both white supremacists and more moderate elements within the Civil Rights Movement. Critics accused Black Power activists of promoting violence and separatism, and the movement's confrontational tactics often sparked backlash from law enforcement and government authorities.

Moreover, internal divisions and ideological differences within the Black Power movement sometimes led to tensions and conflicts among activists. Debates over the role of violence, the relationship between race and class, and the nature of black identity and solidarity often divided the movement and contributed to its eventual decline.

Legacy of the Black Power Movement

Despite its challenges and controversies, the Black Power movement left a lasting legacy that continues to influence social and political movements today. Its emphasis on black pride, self-determination, and community empowerment helped to raise awareness of the deep-seated racism and inequality facing African Americans and inspired generations of activists to continue the fight for justice and equality.

Moreover, the Black Power movement paved the way for greater recognition of African American culture, history, and identity in American society. Its influence can be seen in the rise of black studies programs in universities, the mainstreaming of African American cultural expressions such as music, literature, and art, and the ongoing struggle for racial justice and liberation.

In conclusion, the Black Power movement represented a critical phase in the evolution of the Civil Rights Movement and a powerful assertion of African American agency and resistance. Its principles of self-determination, solidarity, and empowerment continue to resonate with those fighting for justice and equality in contemporary America, providing a framework for addressing the persistent challenges of racism, inequality, and injustice.

Chapter 10: Assassinations and the Movement's Endurance

The assassinations of prominent civil rights leaders such as Martin Luther King Jr., Malcolm X, and others represented devastating blows to the Civil Rights Movement. Yet, despite these tragic losses, the movement demonstrated remarkable resilience in the face of violence and repression. This chapter assesses the impact of the assassinations of key figures, examines the movement's endurance, and explores the legacy of fallen leaders and their enduring influence on the struggle for equality.

Impact of Assassinations

The assassinations of Martin Luther King Jr. and Malcolm X, along with other civil rights leaders, had profound and far-reaching consequences for the Civil Rights Movement. These acts of violence not only robbed the movement of its most charismatic and influential leaders but also created a climate of fear and uncertainty among activists and supporters.

- **Martin Luther King Jr.**: King's assassination on April 4, 1968, in Memphis, Tennessee, sent shockwaves across the country and plunged the Civil Rights Movement into mourning. King's death was a devastating loss for the movement, depriving it of its most prominent and respected leader. His assassination also sparked widespread riots and unrest in cities across America, underscoring the depth of anger and frustration felt by African Americans.

- **Malcolm X**: Malcolm X, a fiery advocate for black nationalism and self-defense, was assassinated on February 21, 1965, while delivering a speech in New York City. His death left a void in the struggle for racial justice and black liberation, depriving the movement of his bold and uncompromising voice. Malcolm's assassination highlighted the dangers faced by those who dared to challenge the status quo and demand radical change.

- **Other Civil Rights Leaders**: The Civil Rights Movement also lost other key figures to assassination, including Medgar Evers, a Mississippi NAACP leader, who was killed in 1963, and Fred Hampton, a leader of the Black Panther

Party, who was killed in a police raid in 1969. These assassinations further underscored the risks and sacrifices involved in the struggle for racial equality.

Resilience of the Movement

Despite the devastating impact of the assassinations, the Civil Rights Movement demonstrated remarkable resilience and continued to press forward in its quest for justice and equality. Activists and organizers across the country refused to be intimidated by violence and repression, and the movement adapted and evolved in response to changing circumstances.

- **Community Organizing**: In the aftermath of the assassinations, grassroots organizations and community leaders stepped up their efforts to mobilize and empower African American communities. Groups like the Southern Christian Leadership Conference (SCLC), the NAACP, and the Congress of Racial Equality (CORE) continued to organize protests, demonstrations, and voter registration drives, keeping the momentum of the movement alive.

- **Youth Activism**: The younger generation of activists, inspired by the legacy of fallen leaders like King and Malcolm X, emerged as a driving force within the Civil Rights Movement. Organizations like the Student Nonviolent Coordinating Committee (SNCC) and the Black Panther Party mobilized young people to take action against racial injustice and inequality, demonstrating the enduring influence of the movement's ideals and principles.

- **International Solidarity**: The Civil Rights Movement also garnered support and solidarity from international allies, who condemned the violence and repression faced by African Americans in the United States. Leaders and organizations from around the world, including Nelson Mandela and the African National Congress in South Africa, expressed solidarity with the struggle for racial equality, highlighting the global significance of the movement.

Legacy of Fallen Leaders

The legacy of fallen leaders such as Martin Luther King Jr., Malcolm X, and others continues to inspire and guide the struggle for equality and justice today. Their courage, vision, and sacrifice serve as a reminder of the ongoing fight against racism and oppression and the importance of collective action and solidarity.

- **Martin Luther King Jr.**: King's commitment to nonviolent resistance and his unwavering dedication to the principles of justice and equality left an indelible mark on the Civil Rights Movement and the broader struggle for human rights. His speeches, writings, and activism continue to inspire activists and organizers around the world, serving as a guiding light in the fight against injustice.

- **Malcolm X**: Malcolm X's critique of white supremacy and his advocacy for black empowerment and self-determination resonated with many African Americans seeking liberation from oppression. His call for black pride and self-reliance continues to influence movements for black liberation and empowerment, challenging mainstream narratives of assimilation and accommodation.

- **Other Civil Rights Leaders**: The contributions of other fallen leaders, such as Medgar Evers and Fred Hampton, are also remembered and honored for their bravery and dedication to the cause of racial justice. Their sacrifices serve as a reminder of the high cost of freedom and the ongoing struggle for equality.

Enduring Influence on the Struggle for Equality

The assassinations of civil rights leaders were tragic and senseless acts of violence that sought to silence voices of dissent and derail the progress of the Civil Rights Movement. However, the movement's endurance in the face of adversity and its continued commitment to justice and equality are a testament to the resilience of the human spirit.

Today, the legacy of the Civil Rights Movement lives on in the ongoing struggle for racial justice and equality. Activists and organizers continue to draw inspiration from the courage and sacrifice of those who came before them, working tirelessly to dismantle systemic racism and build a more just and equitable society for all.

In conclusion, the assassinations of civil rights leaders were painful and traumatic events that deeply affected the Civil Rights Movement. Yet, despite the loss of key figures, the movement persisted, demonstrating remarkable resilience and enduring influence. The legacy of fallen leaders continues to inspire and guide the struggle for equality and justice, reminding us of the importance of perseverance and collective action in the face of oppression.

Chapter 11: Affirmative Action and Continuing Challenges

Affirmative action policies have been a central component of efforts to address historical inequalities and promote diversity and inclusion in education, employment, and other areas. However, these policies have also been the subject of intense legal battles and debates about their effectiveness and fairness. This chapter provides an overview of affirmative action policies, examines the legal challenges they have faced, and explores ongoing challenges to racial equality in education, employment, and other areas.

Overview of Affirmative Action

Affirmative action refers to policies and programs designed to address past and present discrimination by providing opportunities and preferences to individuals from groups that have historically been disadvantaged or underrepresented. These policies aim to promote diversity, equity, and inclusion in institutions and workplaces, thereby creating a more level playing field for all.

In the United States, affirmative action policies have been implemented in various sectors, including education, employment, government contracting, and housing. These policies may take the form of outreach and recruitment efforts, preferential treatment in admissions or hiring decisions, or the establishment of goals and timetables for achieving diversity and representation.

Legal Battles and Debates

Affirmative action policies have been the subject of numerous legal challenges, with opponents arguing that they amount to reverse discrimination and violate the principle of equal treatment under the law. The Supreme Court has issued several landmark decisions on affirmative action, shaping the legal framework for its implementation and enforcement.

- **Regents of the University of California v. Bakke (1978):** In this case, the Supreme Court ruled that quotas based on race were unconstitutional but upheld the use of race as one of several factors in admissions decisions, affirming the constitutionality of affirmative action in higher education.

- **Grutter v. Bollinger (2003) and Gratz v. Bollinger (2003):** These cases involved challenges to the University of Michigan's affirmative action policies. The Supreme Court upheld the law school's policy, which considered race as one of many factors in admissions, while striking down the undergraduate admissions policy, which awarded points based on race.

- **Fisher v. University of Texas at Austin (2013, 2016):** These cases involved challenges to the University of Texas at Austin's use of race as a factor in admissions. The Supreme Court upheld the university's admissions policy, ruling that it was narrowly tailored to achieve diversity and did not violate the Constitution's equal protection clause.

Effectiveness and Fairness

Debates about the effectiveness and fairness of affirmative action policies continue to rage, with proponents arguing that they are necessary to address systemic inequalities and promote diversity, while opponents argue that they perpetuate racial preferences and undermine merit-based principles.

- **Effectiveness:** Proponents of affirmative action point to research showing that diversity in educational and workplace settings benefits all members of the community by fostering creativity, innovation, and critical thinking. They argue that affirmative action policies help to break down barriers and create opportunities for historically marginalized groups to succeed.

- **Fairness:** Opponents of affirmative action argue that it is inherently unfair to give preferential treatment to individuals based on their race or ethnicity, regardless of historical injustices. They argue that affirmative action policies discriminate against individuals who may have worked hard and achieved success on their own merits, regardless of their race or background.

Ongoing Challenges to Racial Equality

Despite the existence of affirmative action policies, significant challenges to racial equality persist in education, employment, and other areas. Structural barriers, institutionalized racism, and unconscious bias continue to limit opportunities for African Americans and other marginalized groups, perpetuating cycles of inequality and disadvantage.

- **Education**: Racial disparities in access to quality education remain a persistent problem, with African American and Hispanic students disproportionately attending underfunded schools with fewer resources and opportunities. Affirmative action policies in higher education have faced backlash from critics who argue that they unfairly advantage some students over others.

- **Employment**: African Americans continue to face discrimination in the workplace, with studies showing that they are less likely to be hired, promoted, or paid fairly compared to their white counterparts. Affirmative action policies aimed at promoting diversity in the workforce have faced legal challenges and opposition from employers who argue that they infringe on their rights.

- **Criminal Justice:** The criminal justice system disproportionately targets and incarcerates African Americans, leading to widespread disparities in arrest rates, sentencing outcomes, and rates of incarceration. Affirmative action policies aimed at addressing these disparities have faced resistance from law enforcement agencies and policymakers who argue that they undermine public safety and the rule of law.

Conclusion

Affirmative action policies have been a contentious and hotly debated issue in American society, with proponents and opponents offering divergent views on their effectiveness and fairness. While affirmative action has helped to promote diversity and inclusion in education, employment, and other areas, significant challenges to racial equality persist.

Moving forward, addressing these challenges will require a multi-faceted approach that includes not only affirmative action policies but also broader efforts to dismantle systemic racism, promote equity and inclusion, and address the root causes of inequality. By working together to confront these issues head-on, we can build a more just and equitable society for all.

Chapter 12: Intersectionality and the Expansion of Civil Rights

Intersectionality has emerged as a critical framework for understanding the complexities of discrimination and oppression, recognizing that individuals experience multiple forms of discrimination based on their intersecting identities, such as race, gender, sexuality, and disability. This chapter explores the concept of intersectionality and its importance, examines how the Civil Rights Movement paved the way for broader struggles for gender, LGBTQ+, and disability rights, and profiles intersectional activists who fought for justice on multiple fronts.

Understanding Intersectionality

Intersectionality, coined by legal scholar Kimberlé Crenshaw in the late 1980s, acknowledges that individuals experience intersecting forms of discrimination and privilege based on their multiple social identities. It recognizes that racism, sexism, homophobia, transphobia, ableism, and other forms of oppression are interconnected and mutually reinforcing.

At its core, intersectionality challenges simplistic understandings of identity and discrimination, urging us to consider the ways in which race, gender, sexuality, class, disability, and other factors intersect and shape individuals' experiences and opportunities. It highlights the importance of addressing these intersecting forms of oppression in order to achieve true equality and justice for all.

The Civil Rights Movement and Intersectionality

The Civil Rights Movement played a pivotal role in laying the groundwork for broader struggles for social justice and equality by challenging institutionalized racism and segregation. However, it also laid bare the limitations of a singular focus on race, as African American women, LGBTQ+ individuals, and people with disabilities faced intersecting forms of discrimination within the movement itself.

- **Women in the Civil Rights Movement**: African American women played crucial roles in the Civil Rights Movement, serving as leaders, organizers, and activists. Yet, they often faced marginalization and sexism within the movement, as their contributions were overshadowed by those of their male counterparts. Women like Ella Baker, Fannie Lou Hamer, and Diane Nash challenged gender norms and advocated for gender equality within the movement.

- **LGBTQ+ Activism**: While LGBTQ+ issues were not central to the Civil Rights Movement, the struggle for racial justice laid the groundwork for broader movements for LGBTQ+ rights. LGBTQ+ activists drew inspiration from the tactics and strategies of the Civil Rights Movement, organizing protests, demonstrations, and advocacy campaigns to challenge discrimination and promote equality.

- **Disability Rights**: People with disabilities also faced discrimination and marginalization within the Civil Rights Movement, as they were often excluded from participation due to physical barriers and social stigma. Disability rights activists, such as Ed Roberts and Judy Heumann, drew on the principles of the Civil Rights Movement to advocate for equal rights and opportunities for people with disabilities.

Intersectional Activists

Throughout history, intersectional activists have fought for justice on multiple fronts, challenging systems of oppression and advocating for the rights and dignity of marginalized communities. These activists have recognized the interconnected nature of discrimination and oppression and have worked tirelessly to address the root causes of inequality.

- **Audre Lorde**: Audre Lorde was a poet, writer, and activist who addressed issues of race, gender, sexuality, and class in her work. She coined the term "intersectionality" and emphasized the importance of recognizing the ways in which different forms of oppression intersect and compound each other. Lorde's activism centered on empowering marginalized communities and amplifying their voices.

- **Marsha P. Johnson**: Marsha P. Johnson was a transgender activist and one of the leaders of the Stonewall uprising in 1969, which is widely regarded as the catalyst for the modern LGBTQ+ rights movement. Johnson fought tirelessly for the rights of transgender and gender-nonconforming people, advocating for visibility, acceptance, and equality.

- **Melba Pattillo Beals**: Melba Pattillo Beals was one of the Little Rock Nine, a group of African American students who desegregated Central High School in Little Rock, Arkansas, in 1957. As a Black woman, Beals faced intersecting forms of discrimination based on race and gender, yet she remained steadfast in her commitment to achieving equality and justice for all.

The Legacy of Intersectional Activism

The legacy of intersectional activism continues to shape social justice movements today, as activists and organizers recognize the importance of addressing intersecting forms of oppression and discrimination. Intersectionality has become a central tenet of contemporary social justice movements, informing strategies and tactics aimed at challenging systemic inequality and promoting inclusion and equity.

By centering the experiences and voices of marginalized communities and recognizing the interconnected nature of discrimination and oppression, intersectional activists are working to build a more just and equitable world for all. Their efforts remind us of the importance of solidarity, allyship, and collective action in the fight for social justice and equality.

In conclusion, intersectionality has emerged as a powerful framework for understanding the complexities of discrimination and oppression and addressing the intersecting forms of inequality that shape individuals' lives. The Civil Rights Movement paved the way for broader struggles for gender, LGBTQ+, and disability rights by challenging institutionalized racism and segregation, while intersectional activists continue to fight for justice on multiple fronts, recognizing the interconnected nature of oppression and discrimination.

Chapter 13: Reckoning with the Past: Truth and Reconciliation

Efforts to confront the legacy of slavery, segregation, and systemic racism in America have sparked a national reckoning with the country's racial history. This chapter delves into the discussion of these efforts, examining truth and reconciliation initiatives aimed at acknowledging past injustices and promoting healing. It also explores the challenges and controversies surrounding the reckoning with America's racial history.

Confronting America's Racial Past

The United States has a long and troubled history of racial injustice, stemming from centuries of slavery, followed by segregation, discrimination, and systemic racism. Despite significant strides toward racial equality, the legacy of this history continues to shape contemporary society, manifesting in racial disparities in wealth, education, healthcare, and criminal justice.

Efforts to confront America's racial past have gained momentum in recent years, driven by a growing recognition of the need to acknowledge and address the enduring effects of historical injustices. From grassroots activism to institutional initiatives, individuals and organizations are seeking to uncover the truth about America's racial history and promote healing and reconciliation.

Truth and Reconciliation Initiatives

Truth and reconciliation initiatives aim to address historical injustices by acknowledging past wrongs, promoting dialogue and understanding, and fostering healing and reconciliation among affected communities. These initiatives draw inspiration from similar efforts in other countries, such as South Africa, where the Truth and Reconciliation Commission played a pivotal role in the country's transition from apartheid to democracy.

In the United States, truth and reconciliation initiatives have taken various forms, including:

- **Historical Research and Documentation:** Scholars, researchers, and historians are engaged in efforts to uncover and document the full extent of America's racial history, including the legacies of slavery, segregation, and systemic racism. Their work seeks to provide a comprehensive understanding of the root causes and consequences of racial injustice.

- **Community Dialogues and Healing Circles:** Community-based organizations and grassroots activists are organizing dialogues, forums, and healing circles to facilitate conversations about America's racial history and its impact on individuals and communities. These spaces provide opportunities for reflection, dialogue, and mutual understanding, fostering empathy and compassion among participants.

- **Public Memorials and Commemorations:** Public memorials, monuments, and commemorations play a crucial role in acknowledging and honoring the victims of racial violence and injustice. From lynching memorials to Civil Rights Movement landmarks, these sites serve as reminders of America's troubled past and the ongoing struggle for racial justice.

- **Policy Reform and Redress:** Truth and reconciliation initiatives often include calls for policy reform and redress measures aimed at addressing the lingering effects of historical injustices. This may include reparations for descendants of enslaved Africans, reforms to criminal justice systems, and investments in communities disproportionately affected by racism and inequality.

Challenges and Controversies

Despite the noble intentions behind truth and reconciliation initiatives, they are not without challenges and controversies. Some of the key challenges include:

- **Resistance and Denial:** Efforts to confront America's racial past are often met with resistance and denial from individuals and institutions that are unwilling to acknowledge the reality of historical injustices. This resistance can hinder progress toward reconciliation and healing, perpetuating cycles of harm and injustice.

- **Political Polarization:** America's racial history is deeply intertwined with politics, and efforts to address it can become politicized, leading to divisions and polarization. Partisan rhetoric and ideological differences may impede constructive dialogue and collaboration, making it difficult to find common ground and move forward.

- **Limitations of Legal Frameworks**: Truth and reconciliation initiatives face limitations within the existing legal frameworks, which may not provide adequate mechanisms for addressing historical injustices. Legal barriers, such as statutes of limitations and immunity laws, can hinder efforts to hold perpetrators of past atrocities accountable and provide restitution to victims.

- **Unequal Access to Resources**: Marginalized communities, particularly communities of color, may face barriers to participating in truth and reconciliation initiatives due to unequal access to resources and opportunities. Lack of funding, infrastructure, and support can hinder the meaningful engagement of affected communities in the process of reconciliation and healing.

Conclusion

The reckoning with America's racial past is an essential step toward building a more just, equitable, and inclusive society. Truth and reconciliation initiatives offer opportunities to acknowledge past wrongs, promote healing and reconciliation, and pave the way for a more hopeful future. However, they also face significant challenges and controversies that must be addressed in order to achieve meaningful progress.

By confronting the legacy of slavery, segregation, and systemic racism head-on, and by engaging in honest dialogue and reflection, we can begin to dismantle the structures of oppression and injustice that continue to shape our society. The path to truth and reconciliation may be long and difficult, but it is essential for building a more just and equitable world for future generations.

Chapter 14: Contemporary Civil Rights Movements

In the 21st century, civil rights movements continue to shape the social and political landscape, challenging systemic injustices and advocating for equality, justice, and human rights. This chapter provides an overview of recent civil rights movements, including Black Lives Matter and campaigns against police brutality, examines the tactics, goals, and impact of contemporary activism, and explores intersectional alliances and coalitions working toward social justice in the modern era.

The Rise of Black Lives Matter

The Black Lives Matter (BLM) movement emerged in response to the acquittal of George Zimmerman, the man who fatally shot Trayvon Martin, an unarmed black teenager, in 2012. Founded by Alicia Garza, Patrisse Cullors, and Opal Tometi, BLM quickly gained momentum as a grassroots movement advocating for an end to police brutality and systemic racism.

- **Tactics**: BLM employs a variety of tactics, including protests, demonstrations, direct action, social media campaigns, and community organizing. The movement gained widespread attention for its use of hashtags such as #BlackLivesMatter and #SayHerName to raise awareness of police violence and amplify the voices of those affected.

- **Goals**: The primary goal of BLM is to end the disproportionate violence and discrimination faced by black communities at the hands of law enforcement. The movement also advocates for systemic reforms, including changes to policing practices, criminal justice reform, and investments in community-based solutions to violence and inequality.

- **Impact**: BLM has had a significant impact on public discourse and policy debates surrounding race and policing. The movement has helped to elevate issues of police brutality and racial injustice to the national stage, prompting widespread protests, reforms, and calls for accountability. BLM has also inspired solidarity movements around the world, drawing attention to racial injustices in other countries.

Campaigns Against Police Brutality

In addition to BLM, there have been numerous campaigns and movements focused specifically on combating police brutality and misconduct. These movements often arise in response to high-profile cases of police violence against black, brown, and marginalized communities.

- **Say Her Name**: The Say Her Name movement, initiated by the African American Policy Forum, seeks to raise awareness of police violence against black women and girls. The campaign highlights the stories of women like Sandra Bland, Breonna Taylor, and Atatiana Jefferson, who have been killed by police officers.

- **Campaign Zero**: Campaign Zero is a policy-oriented movement founded by activists associated with BLM. The campaign focuses on advocating for concrete policy solutions to end police violence, including demilitarization of police forces, de-escalation training, and community oversight of law enforcement agencies.

- **ACLU's Campaign for Smart Justice**: The American Civil Liberties Union (ACLU) has been at the forefront of efforts to combat police brutality and mass incarceration. The organization's Campaign for Smart Justice advocates for reforms to policing and criminal justice systems, with a focus on ending racial disparities and promoting fairness and accountability.

Intersectional Alliances and Coalitions

Contemporary civil rights movements have increasingly embraced intersectionality, recognizing the interconnected nature of oppression and the importance of building alliances across diverse communities. Intersectional alliances and coalitions bring together activists and organizations working on various social justice issues, including race, gender, sexuality, disability, and immigration.

- **The Movement for Black Lives**: The Movement for Black Lives (M4BL) is a coalition of over 150 organizations committed to advocating for black liberation and racial justice. M4BL's platform encompasses a wide range of issues, including criminal justice reform, economic justice, environmental justice, and LGBTQ+ rights.

- **The Women's March**: The Women's March, initiated in 2017 in response to the inauguration of President Donald Trump, brought together millions of people around the world to protest against misogyny, racism, and other forms of oppression. The movement has emphasized intersectionality and solidarity, amplifying the voices of women of color, LGBTQ+ individuals, and other marginalized groups.

- **The Poor People's Campaign**: Reviving the spirit of Dr. Martin Luther King Jr.'s original Poor People's Campaign, the contemporary movement seeks to address the intersecting issues of poverty, racism, ecological devastation, and militarism. Led by Reverend Dr. William Barber II and Reverend Dr. Liz Theoharis, the campaign mobilizes people across racial, ethnic, and socioeconomic lines to demand systemic change.

Challenges and Opportunities

While contemporary civil rights movements have made significant strides in raising awareness, mobilizing communities, and advocating for change, they also face challenges and obstacles. These challenges include:

- **Resistance and Backlash**: Civil rights movements often face resistance and backlash from entrenched power structures, including law enforcement agencies, political leaders, and conservative media outlets. Efforts to challenge systemic racism and inequality may be met with hostility, repression, and violence.

- **Internal Divisions**: Like any social movement, civil rights movements are not immune to internal divisions and conflicts. Differences in tactics, strategies, and priorities may lead to tensions and disagreements within activist communities, potentially undermining unity and effectiveness.

- **Co-Optation and Dilution**: There is a risk that mainstream institutions and corporations may seek to co-opt and dilute the message and goals of civil rights movements for their own purposes. Activists must remain vigilant and critical of attempts to commodify and depoliticize the movement's demands for justice and equality.

Despite these challenges, contemporary civil rights movements offer opportunities for meaningful change and transformation. By centering the experiences and voices of marginalized communities, building intersectional alliances, and mobilizing collective action, these movements have the potential to challenge systemic oppression and build a more just and equitable society for all.

In conclusion, contemporary civil rights movements like Black Lives Matter and campaigns against police brutality continue to shape the social and political landscape, advocating for racial justice, human rights, and systemic change. These movements employ a variety of tactics, embrace intersectionality, and build alliances across diverse communities, challenging systemic injustices and working toward a more inclusive and equitable future.

Chapter 15: Looking Ahead: Challenges and Opportunities

As we look ahead to the future of civil rights and the ongoing struggle for equality, it is essential to assess the current state of affairs, confront emerging challenges, and reflect on the lessons of the past. This chapter examines the current landscape of civil rights, discusses emerging challenges such as voter suppression and the resurgence of white supremacy, and offers reflections on the lessons of the Civil Rights Movement and the prospects for a more just and inclusive future.

The Current State of Civil Rights

While significant progress has been made in advancing civil rights and promoting equality, systemic injustices and inequalities persist, disproportionately impacting marginalized communities, including people of color, LGBTQ+ individuals, immigrants, and people with disabilities. Racial disparities persist in areas such as education, healthcare, housing, and criminal justice, highlighting the ongoing need for systemic change.

- **Racial Injustice:** Systemic racism continues to shape all aspects of American society, from policing and criminal justice to education, employment, and healthcare. African Americans and other communities of color face disproportionate rates of police violence, mass incarceration, economic inequality, and lack of access to quality services and opportunities.

- **LGBTQ+ Rights**: Despite significant gains in LGBTQ+ rights, including marriage equality and anti-discrimination protections, LGBTQ+ individuals still face discrimination, harassment, and violence in many areas of life. Transgender and gender-nonconforming people, in particular, face high rates of violence, discrimination, and lack of access to healthcare and social services.

- **Immigrant Rights**: Immigrants, especially undocumented immigrants, face discrimination, exploitation, and harsh treatment under immigration policies that criminalize and scapegoat them. The rights of asylum seekers, refugees, and immigrant communities are under threat, with policies aimed at restricting immigration and demonizing immigrants.

- **Disability Rights**: People with disabilities continue to face barriers to full participation in society, including lack of access to transportation, employment, education, and public accommodations. Discrimination and stigma persist, limiting opportunities for people with disabilities to live independently and contribute to their communities.

Emerging Challenges

In addition to longstanding issues of inequality and injustice, new challenges have emerged in recent years, posing threats to civil rights and social progress. These challenges include:

- **Voter Suppression**: Efforts to suppress voting rights, particularly targeting communities of color, young people, and low-income individuals, threaten to undermine the democratic process and disenfranchise millions of voters. Voter ID laws, gerrymandering, purges of voter rolls, and restrictions on early voting and absentee ballots disproportionately impact marginalized communities.

- **Resurgence of White Supremacy**: The rise of white supremacist ideology and hate groups poses a significant threat to civil rights and social cohesion. Hate crimes targeting racial and religious minorities, immigrants, LGBTQ+ individuals, and other marginalized groups have surged in recent years, fueled by xenophobia, racism, and intolerance.

- **Erosion of Civil Liberties**: The erosion of civil liberties and constitutional rights, including freedom of speech, assembly, and the press, undermines democratic principles and threatens the ability of activists and marginalized communities to advocate for change. Surveillance, censorship, and crackdowns on dissent stifle voices of dissent and undermine efforts to challenge injustice.

- **Global Threats to Human Rights**: Internationally, human rights are under attack in many parts of the world, with authoritarian regimes and oppressive governments cracking down on civil liberties, persecuting activists and dissidents, and perpetuating violence and repression. The global rise of authoritarianism poses a threat to democracy, peace, and human dignity.

Reflections on the Lessons of the Civil Rights Movement

In confronting these challenges, it is essential to reflect on the lessons of the Civil Rights Movement and draw inspiration from the courage, resilience, and determination of those who came before us. The Civil Rights Movement offers valuable insights into effective strategies for social change, including:

- **Nonviolent Resistance**: The Civil Rights Movement demonstrated the power of nonviolent resistance as a means of challenging injustice and mobilizing communities for change. The tactics of sit-ins, boycotts, marches, and civil disobedience were instrumental in raising awareness, mobilizing public support, and pressuring policymakers to enact reforms.

- **Coalition Building**: The Civil Rights Movement brought together diverse communities and organizations, including African Americans, whites, students, religious groups, labor unions, and grassroots activists, to work toward a common goal of racial justice and equality. Building alliances across lines of race, class, and ideology was crucial to the success of the movement.

- **Strategic Litigation**: Strategic litigation played a significant role in advancing civil rights and challenging discriminatory laws and practices. Organizations like the NAACP Legal Defense Fund used the courts to challenge segregation and discrimination, securing landmark victories such as Brown v. Board of Education and the Civil Rights Act of 1964.

- **Long-Term Commitment**: The Civil Rights Movement was a long-term struggle that required sustained commitment, dedication, and perseverance. Activists and organizers worked tirelessly for years, facing setbacks, obstacles, and violence, but never losing sight of their ultimate goal of justice and equality.

Prospects for a More Just and Inclusive Future

Despite the challenges and obstacles ahead, there are reasons for hope and optimism as we look to the future of civil rights and social justice. Grassroots movements, community organizations, and advocacy groups continue to mobilize and organize for change, challenging injustice and advocating for a more just and inclusive society.

- **Youth Activism**: The youth-led movements of today, including the Sunrise Movement, March for Our Lives, and Fridays for Future, demonstrate the power of young people to drive social change and advocate for a better future. Youth activists are leading the fight against gun violence, climate change, racial injustice, and other pressing issues, bringing fresh energy, creativity, and urgency to the struggle for civil rights and social justice.

- **Intersectional Advocacy**: Intersectional advocacy has become increasingly central to contemporary social justice movements, recognizing the interconnected nature of oppression and the importance of addressing multiple forms of discrimination and inequality. Activists and organizations are working across lines of race, gender, sexuality, class, and other identities to build inclusive movements that center the experiences and needs of marginalized communities.

- **Global Solidarity**: The fight for civil rights and social justice is increasingly interconnected with global struggles for human rights and liberation. Solidarity movements are emerging that transcend national boundaries, linking activists and organizations across the world in common cause against oppression, exploitation, and injustice. From the Arab Spring to the Black Lives Matter movement, global solidarity has become a powerful force for change.

- **Policy Reform and Structural Change**: Calls for systemic change and structural reform are gaining momentum, with demands for policies that address root causes of inequality and injustice. Campaigns for police reform, criminal justice reform, economic justice, healthcare reform, and environmental justice are pushing for transformative policies that promote equity, dignity, and human rights for all.

- **Civic Engagement and Advocacy**: Civic engagement and advocacy are essential tools for advancing civil rights and social justice, empowering individuals and communities to participate in the democratic process and hold policymakers accountable. Voting, community organizing, lobbying, and grassroots activism are vital means of effecting change and shaping the future of society.

In conclusion, while the challenges ahead are daunting, the prospects for a more just and inclusive future are within reach. By drawing on the lessons of the past, mobilizing collective action, and building alliances across diverse communities, we can confront systemic injustice, dismantle oppressive structures, and create a society that upholds the principles of equality, justice, and human rights for all. The struggle for civil rights and social justice is ongoing, but with perseverance, solidarity, and determination, we can build a better world for future generations.

Don't miss out!

Visit the website below and you can sign up to receive emails whenever Michael Johnson publishes a new book. There's no charge and no obligation.

https://books2read.com/r/B-A-OREFB-AJIAD

BOOKS 2 READ

Connecting independent readers to independent writers.

Did you love *The Civil Rights Movement*? Then you should read *American Chronicles*[1] by Michael Johnson!

[2]

"American Chronicles: A History of the United States" offers a comprehensive journey through the pivotal moments that shaped the nation. From the rich tapestry of indigenous civilizations to the tumultuous struggles of the Civil Rights Movement and beyond, this book explores the key events, figures, and themes that define American history. From the Revolutionary War to the Cold War and beyond, witness the rise of a nation, the trials of war, and the ongoing quest for equality and freedom. Experience the story of America, from its origins to its enduring legacy in the modern world.

---

1. https://books2read.com/u/3y9qLL

2. https://books2read.com/u/3y9qLL

About the Author

Michael Johnson is a distinguished historian specializing in American history. With a degree in History from Harvard University, Johnson's work delves into pivotal moments, figures, and themes shaping the United States. He has authored numerous acclaimed books, offering insightful perspectives and engaging narratives. Johnson's commitment to meticulous scholarship and compelling storytelling has earned him widespread acclaim in the field. Passionate about sharing his expertise, he frequently engages in lectures and public events to foster a deeper appreciation for America's past.